D1128500

The FIRST BOOK of

WOOL

The FIRST BOOK of

WOOL

Betty Cavanna
&
George Russell Harrison

Illustrated with photographs

FRANKLIN WATTS INC.
575 Lexington Ave.
New York, N.Y. 10022

ACKNOWLEDGMENTS

We are grateful to friends who helped us in gathering material for this book.

Sir Frederick White, head of the Australian Commonwealth Scientific and Industrial Research Organization, arranged our introduction to the wool industry of that country, and Mr. Brian McKeon of the Melbourne office of CSIRO helped us get acquainted with it. Mr. and Mrs. H. N. Hopkins of Wormbeat, Winchelsea, Victoria, opened the hospitality of one of the oldest Australian sheep farms, even to having two unfortunate rams sheared out of season so that we might photograph the operation.

Some pictures came from the Australian Wool Bureau of CSIRO, and some from the Information Branch of the Victorian Department of Agriculture. We are grateful also for the photographs furnished through the kindness of John Fitzgerald of the Publicity Department of Dalgarty and New Zealand Loan Ltd. of Sydney, Australia.

Much valuable material was sent us by Dr. Gerald Laxer and Mr. Raymond Keys of the International Wool Secretariat, London, England, and numerous photographs were furnished by the Wool Bureau, Inc., of New York City.

Other illustrations were supplied through the kindness of Dr. Harold P. Lundgren, Chief of the Wool and Mohair Laboratory of the U. S. Department of Agriculture in Albany, California, who was most helpful in answering questions and directing us to sources of information. Photographs were also furnished by the Office of Information, U. S. Department of Agriculture.

Other photographs were furnished by Robert Bowden of the Felters' Company of Millbury, Massachusetts, who showed us the complete operation of a modern felt factory.

Still others were provided by the Merrimack Valley Textile Museum of North Andover, Massachusetts, to whose director, James C. Hippen, we are grateful for information and for permission to take photographs.

Our special thanks go to Professor Stanley Backer, head of the Textile Division of the Massachusetts Institute of Technology, who introduced us to the story of wool, and Professor A. B. MacNamara, who kindly reviewed the manuscript.

CONTENTS

The FIRST BOOK of

WOOL

A flock of Merino sheep on an Australian hillside. (AUSTRALIAN WOOL BUREAU)

WHAT IS WOOL?

EVER SINCE MEN became civilized, wool has been important to them. At times in history, wool has been more valuable than gold, and at other times men have fought for the land on which to raise sheep. Some ranchers have grown rich through wool, while others have starved.

Right now, on the grassy plains of Australia, in the high Andes Mountains of Peru, on the slopes of the Kashmir mountains between India and Pakistan, in the hills of Scotland, and in many other places, shepherds are watching their flocks of sheep or goats or llamas. Sometime during the coming year the coats of these animals will be sheared for wool, which will be made into clothing or blankets or carpets for people who may live hundreds or thousands of miles away.

Most of the clothing we wear is fashioned from cloth woven from threads called yarns, which are made by twisting short fibers together so tightly that they cling to each other and are hard to pull apart. Many kinds of fibers, including cotton, linen, silk, and wool are strong and flexible enough to make good yarn.

This is how a twisted strand of yarn looks through a microscope. The twist makes the fibers hang together. (BRITISH WOOL BUREAU)

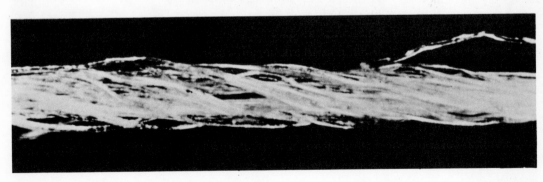

1

Cotton fibers grow on the seeds of the cotton plant, where they act as tiny sails that help the wind scatter the seeds far and wide. Linen fibers are a part of the stalks of the flax plant, which they make strong and rigid so that these stalks will not break in the wind. Silk fibers are long filaments of dried plastic material which silkworms spin around themselves to make cocoons. Wool is fine fibers of the hair that grows on sheep and some other animals.

Wool fibers are especially valuable because the yarn they make can be woven into cloth that is soft, warm, light, and strong. Although wool is a kind of hair, it differs from the hair that grows on a person's head

Ends of hair and wool fibers cut and viewed end on, through a microscope. The round fibers are straight; the oval ones are curly. (MERRIMACK VALLEY TEXTILE MUSEUM)

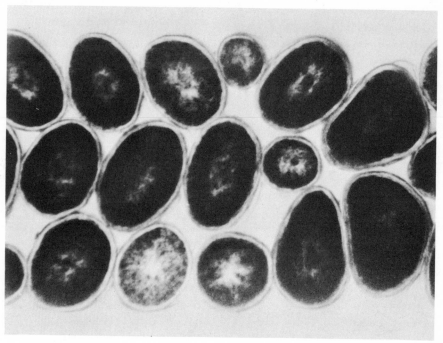

because it is finer and curlier. By looking at its fibers you can see why wool makes such good cloth. Pull a single fiber out of a piece of woolen yarn and you will see that it looks like a fine, crinkly hair. Wool and hair are made of a substance called keratin, which also forms the chemical basis of toenails, horns, and hooves.

Looking at a wool fiber and a hair from a horse's tail together under a microscope shows why one of them is crimped and the other is straight. If we cut both fibers right across with a knife and look at the cut ends under a microscope, we can see that the straight hair fiber is round, while the curly hair fiber is oval and uneven. An oval fiber bends sideways as it comes out of the hole in the skin in which it is formed, and it becomes curved and crinkled. If it is stretched, it will spring back again to its original shape. A round hair grows straight.

Curly or kinky fibers make warmer cloth than straight fibers do. When a cold wind blows against our bodies it takes heat from them, so we put on a woolen sweater or overcoat to keep warm. The thicker and fuzzier this covering, the less the wind can penetrate it and the less heat will be lost through it. It is not the fibers in a piece of cloth that keep heat from passing through, so much as it is the tiny pockets of air held between them. The thousands of air pockets in a fluffy woolen fabric prevent heat from escaping rapidly.

If you pull a wool fiber straight and then pull still harder, you can usually stretch it farther before it breaks. Although wool will not stretch nearly as much as rubber, it is quite elastic. This elasticity increases the strength of cloth made from wool, for it can yield before a force that might otherwise tear it, and then spring back into shape when the force is removed.

Wool fibers are flexible as well as strong, and are not easily broken by being bent. In one experiment, single fibers of wool were bent 20,000 times without breaking, while cotton fibers could be bent only 3,200 times, silk only 1,800, and a man-made plastic of an inferior type only 75 times.

A greatly enlarged photograph (electron microscope) of a wool fiber, showing the scales with which it is covered. (U. S. DEPT. OF AGRICULTURE WOOL AND MOHAIR LABORATORY)

The thinner wool fibers are, the more flexible and strong will be the yarn made from them. The curlier they are, the warmer and fluffier will be the cloth woven of their yarn.

All wool fibers are covered with tiny scales, which cling together when the yarn is stretched, so making it stronger. Hair is also covered with such scales, but the scales on wool are larger and more prominent. The picture on this page shows these microscopic scales. They serve a useful function when the wool is growing on the sheep. Each scale has its loose end pointing toward the free tip of the fiber. Pieces of dirt that get on the fiber are gradually worked out along it by means of the scales.

Many animals have two kinds of hair in their coats: an outer layer of long, straight guard hairs that shed the rain and are a protection from thorns and burrs, and an inner layer of matted curly hair that shuts out the wind and cold and helps insulate the animal by keeping his body heat from escaping into the atmosphere. Thousands of years ago all sheep had long, straight hair with kinky wool underneath. Clothmakers found that the undercoat made better cloth than the long hair did. For shearing, sheep raisers learned to select the animals with the woolliest undercoats, and to use the animals with the least wool for meat. The lambs of the woolliest sheep were likely to be more woolly than the others, also. As a result of many years of such selection, varieties of sheep have been developed for woolgrowing that have no straight hair at all, but are covered entirely with soft, crinkly fibers.

4

The coarse guard hairs of this South American llama cover its wool, which can be seen thrusting through on the right side of the picture. (GEORGE RUSSELL HARRISON)

A Rocky Mountain sheep, which has almost no wool. (MERRIMACK VALLEY TEXTILE MUSEUM)

ANIMALS ON WHICH FLEECE GROWS

MORE THAN 700 million sheep are now being raised for wool. Each year they grow more than 5,000 million pounds of wool — enough to make a thread that would stretch back and forth between the earth and the moon half a million times. But sheep are not the only animals with hair that can be knit or woven into cloth. The silky yarn for angora sweaters is spun from the long, curly fleece of Angora goats, which originally came from Asia Minor. Yarn for fine cashmere shawls is obtained from smaller goats whose ancestors came from Kashmir, north of India.

Several South American relatives of the camel produce woolly hair used to make special kinds of fabric. The llama, which stands four or five feet high at the shoulder, is used as a pack animal by the Indians of Peru. It produces a rather coarse fleece, used to make blankets and rugs. The alpaca and its wild cousin the guanaco are somewhat smaller than the llama. Their wool is famous for its lightness and its fine wearing qualities. More than a million and a half alpacas are sheared every year in the mountains of Bolivia and Peru, and their fleece is sent to factories in the United States and Europe.

The smallest of the South American camel relatives, the vicuña, has

A group of llamas in Peru.

A guanaco of Argentina.

the softest fleece of all. Its fibers are so fine that three million of them can be crowded side by side into a round pipe only an inch wide. Vicuñas are so wild and scarce that cloth made from their hair is probably the most expensive there is. In the days of the Incas, only nobles were permitted to wear vicuña cloth, and the animals could be hunted only once every four years.

A vicuña in the Andes Mountains near Bolivia. (GEORGE RUSSELL HARRISON)

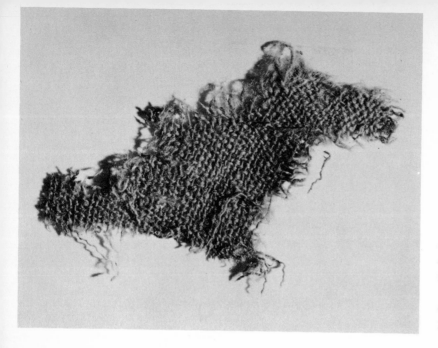

WOOLEN CLOTH IN ANCIENT TIMES

LONG BEFORE MEN became civilized they learned to keep themselves warm by holding around their bodies the skins of animals they had killed for food. Because these skins soon became stiff and smelly, the cave men rubbed them with grease, clay, and salt to soften and preserve them, but they were still heavy and scratchy and uncomfortable to wear.

Later, men learned to make cloth by weaving fibers together. Because this material was lighter and more porous than leather, the perspiration from the body could quickly evaporate, and so men found such clothing more comfortable. For many years, men simply draped long pieces of cloth around their bodies to keep themselves warm when the weather was cold, and cool when it was hot. Then they learned to cut pieces of cloth into irregular shapes and sew them together to make robes and gowns that fitted their bodies more closely.

The fibers used in making the first cloth were not very strong, and the fabric was easily torn. Then gradually people learned that a pinch of

8

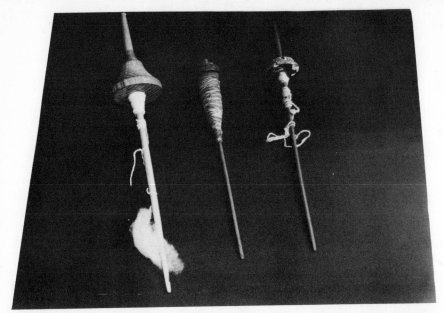

A group of antique spindles. The one on the right was being used by American Indians before Columbus discovered America. (MERRIMACK VALLEY TEXTILE MUSEUM)

short fibers could be twisted into a thread of any length needed, for the fibers held together, with each fiber clinging tightly to those which it overlapped.

The process of making threads or yarns by twisting fibers together is called *spinning*. In spinning, fibers are pulled at a uniform rate out of a bundle and are twisted into a thread by a rotating stick called a *spindle*.

Crude spindles that were used by spinners more than six thousand years ago have been found in Egyptian tombs. Usually these spindles were merely sticks about a foot long, notched at one end to catch the thread. The other end, held in a small stone bowl, could be spun rapidly by rubbing it against the spinner's thigh. As the spinning stick twisted the fibers into a thread, this was coiled around the stick.

9

An Inca woman in Peru weaving blankets of wool on a homemade loom. (GEORGE RUSSELL HARRISON)

After a supply of thread had been spun, it was woven into cloth. First, long lengths of thread were stretched parallel in a row on a large wooden frame called a *loom*. Then another long thread attached to a wooden needle was pulled at right angles through these parallel threads, over one and under the next, all the way across the loom. Each interwoven thread was then pushed close against those that had previously been woven in, and by repeating this process thousands of times a length of cloth was produced.

When men needed to protect their bodies from very cold air, it was found that wool made warmer clothing than the other fibers did. By the time the Romans had built their empire two thousand years ago, sheep were being raised for wool all over the known world. What is now Italy was the center of a vast trade in wool. Julius Caesar, the great Roman general, took spinners and weavers and tailors with his army wherever it went. When the Romans invaded Britain in 55 B.C. they found many herds of sheep and a thriving wool industry already there.

Today many of our best clothes are made of wool. Only in the past few centuries has it become customary for people to buy clothing, or

10

even cloth, in a store. Before that, women in every household spun crude fibers into yarn, wove this into cloth, and then cut and sewed the cloth into garments. Before 1840, the making of woolen cloth was the most widely practiced industry in American homes. Even today, in Peru and Bolivia, Indian women carry with them little bags of wool and small hand spindles, and spend every spare moment in twisting wool fibers into threads which they later weave.

About one-tenth of all the fabric used to make clothing today is woven from wool. Wool would be used more widely if it cost less, but since it is expensive, only garments which must give long wear or must feel especially warm or dry or soft are made from wool. As recently as a hundred years ago most people could not afford even overcoats made entirely of wool.

A native weaver of Guatemala adjusting the yarns on his loom.

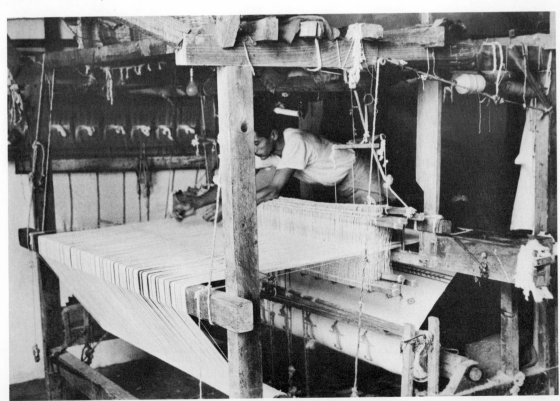

A champion Rambouillet ram. (U. S. DEPT. OF AGRICULTURE OFFICE OF INFORMATION)

RAISING SHEEP FOR WOOL

MOST SHEEP are raised either to produce wool or to furnish meat — mutton or lamb. Although wool can be obtained from sheep which are being raised for meat, different kinds of sheep are ordinarily used for the two purposes.

By mating a ram which has a particularly heavy coat of wool with a ewe whose coat is also heavy, sheep breeders get a certain number of lambs which have heavier coats than either of their parents. When such lambs grow up, the ones with the best coats are mated, and their offspring often have even heavier coats. By repeating this process of selection over and over again, it is possible to breed new varieties of sheep which produce more wool or have finer fleece than ordinary. In this way many important breeds such as the Shetland, Cheviot, Leicester, Rambouillet, and Merino have been developed.

The Merino is the most important wool-bearing breed. While it originated in Spain, it is now the most widely used breed in Australia, where woolgrowing is the country's most important industry. In that land down south of the Equator there are ten times as many sheep as there are people.

A Merino is thickly covered with fine wool from its nose down to its toes. Merinos often have large folds of skin around their necks and shoulders, and these too are covered with wool. When Merino sheep were first being bred, each one gave only three or four pounds of wool at a shearing, but today the average yield has been raised to about ten pounds. A big Merino ram may yield as much as thirty pounds of wool, and champions sometimes yield forty pounds. This amount makes enough cloth for eleven fine woolen suits. It has been estimated that the wool clipped at one shearing from a good Merino ram would make a spun thread long enough to stretch from New York to Chicago.

Breeders are still developing new and better types of sheep for wool production. For instance, some of the best sheep have such thick coats of wool on their faces that they cannot see to eat. To remedy this, breeders have been working to develop an "open-face" sheep that has wool everywhere except on its muzzle.

Prizewinning Merino rams at a Sydney, Australia, sheep show. (DALGARTY AND NEW ZEALAND LOAN, LTD.)

13

Sheep on a ranch in the Sierra Nevada Mountains in Mono National Forest District, near the California line. (EWING GALLOWAY)

Since wool grows thick to keep sheep warm, animals raised where the weather gets quite cold have the best pelts. Yet the climate must not be so cold that sufficient fodder cannot grow. The mountains of Scotland and New Zealand, sections of Australia where a good deal of rain falls, and certain parts of Russia and North America support large numbers of sheep which grow heavy coats.

Sheep can graze on craggy land which is not suitable for raising food for humans or other animals, and still the sheep can produce good wool. They nibble grass so close to its roots that cattle cannot be pastured where sheep have been. In the early days of the American West this situation caused many feuds between cattle raisers and sheep raisers.

Sheep can live on leaves from bushes as well as on grass. Human beings would get indigestion from eating such coarse food, but cows, sheep, goats, camels, and some other animals are *ruminants*. They have stomachs with several compartments, and chew their food more thor-

14

A herd of sheep on the dry land of an Australian sheep station. (ALEX O. COW-PER)

oughly than other animals do. You may have seen a cow or a sheep lying in the shade chewing its cud. The cud is food that the animal has swallowed into the first compartment of its stomach while grazing. Later this food is brought up from the stomach a mouthful at a time, to be chewed again before being swallowed into another stomach compartment. Because a sheep has four stomach compartments it can digest very rough forage.

Unless the pasture is lush, an acre of land or more may be needed to support one sheep the year round. In Australia there are millions of acres that are too dry to grow ordinary crops, but they are covered with bushes and spiky grass which sheep can eat. Sheep ranches in Australia are called stations. On some of the very large ones of up to a million acres, as many as three hundred thousand animals are pastured and fed, and once a year are sheared for wool.

Une fois lan / fait bon ses brebis tondre.
En la saison / sans du cuir escorcher.
Car trop souuent / les peult faire morfondre.
Mes sans le cuir / layne ne croist sur chair.

Sheep shearing — a miniature from the "Three Ages of Man," an unpublished poem attributed to Estienne Porchier. Manuscript of the latter part of the fifteenth century, in the library of M. Ambrose Firmin-Didot, Paris.

TENDING THE FLOCKS

THE OCCUPATION of sheepherder or shepherd goes back to almost the beginnings of history. In the Bible, Psalm 23 begins, "The Lord is my shepherd, I shall not want," and the New Testament, in telling the story of the birth of Jesus, speaks of "shepherds abiding in the field, keeping watch over their flocks by night." Sheepherding was a lonely job, but a respected one.

Often a shepherd had to stay alone with his sheep for weeks at a time, driving them from pasture to pasture and seeing that they did not stray. He also had to protect them from wolves and other wild animals. Where there were no fences, the sheep grazed from one valley or hillside to the next, and often traveled many miles as they slowly ate their way along. Often they were led by a bellwether, an old sheep who knew his way around the pastures and on whose neck a bell was hung so that the other sheep would follow its sound. So, to this day, the word "bellwether" has come to mean "leader."

At night in warm weather the shepherd usually gathered the sheep into a compact flock near his campfire, for the home fold was often too far away to return to except at the end of the season.

In spring, shepherds were busy looking after newborn lambs in the home pastures. Each ewe normally has one lamb a year, but sometimes twins are born. The young lambs are playful, and frisk around their mothers, gamboling with each other and sometimes jumping high in the air.

Lambs with their mothers. (GEORGE RUSSELL HARRISON)

A sheep dog driving a flock of fat lambs out to pasture. (DALGARTY AND NEW ZEALAND LOAN, LTD.)

The shepherd of early days carried a crook, a long staff having at one end an open loop with which he could prod or pull a sheep in the direction he wanted. Later the shepherds trained dogs to round up sheep that were wandering off. The dogs were also company for the shepherds.

Today, with fences to keep sheep from straying and with trucks that can travel miles in a few minutes, the job of the sheepherder is much easier than it once was, but he still needs good sheep dogs to help round up his flock. Over centuries, especially in Scotland, breeds of dogs have been developed that are not only strong and fast, but are also intelligent in handling sheep. A good sheep dog can be trusted to bring back a stray quickly though directed only with a whistle or a gesture. Some well-trained dogs have learned to obey as many as thirty different commands.

It is impressive to see a sheep dog bounding up the side of a steep mountain to circle around an old ewe grazing atop a cliff and in danger of falling, if frightened. The dog is careful not to startle the ewe, but quietly appears in front of her and nudges her gently back to safety.

So strongly have sheepherding instincts been bred into such dogs as the border collie and the kelpie that their tiny untrained puppies can sometimes be seen rounding up flocks of ducks or hens in a barnyard. The modern Scotch collie often shows strong herding instincts, also.

18

A herd of Cheviot sheep in the hills of Scotland. (BRITISH WOOL PROMOTION COMMITTEE)

SHEARING THE FLEECE

SHEARING TIME is usually in the spring, after the weather has become warm enough so that the sheep will not catch cold when they are sheared of their fleecy coats, which are several inches thick.

Even so, a sheep stripped of his heavy wool covering looks very small and chilly. It is no wonder the sheeps' bleating sounds unhappy when they are herded into pens outside the shearing shed. Inside it is a long row of big clippers driven by belts from an electric motor, and waiting beside each clipper is a shearer, a strong and skillful man who travels from one part of the country to another, shearing sheep wherever the weather has become warm enough.

A sheep is delivered to each shearer, who throws it gently to the floor and holds it between his knees while he carefully snips off its coat. First he trims off soiled or scraggly parts of the fleece, then he clips the matted covering of wool from the animal in one piece. So densely packed and entangled are the wool fibers that the fleece usually hangs together like a blanket as it is clipped off.

The shearers who work together in one shed sometimes race to see who can shear the most sheep. A good shearer can clip between 100 and

Australian sheep in pens outside the shed, waiting to be sheared. (VICTORIAN DEPT. OF AGRICULTURE)

This sheep is about to be sheared. (GEORGE RUSSELL HARRISON)

The same sheep three minutes later. His woolly overcoat is on the floor. (GEORGE RUSSELL HARRISON)

A row of shearers working with their power clippers in the shearing shed.
(AUSTRALIAN WOOL BUREAU)

Dipping the sheep after shearing. (VICTORIAN DEPT. OF AGRICULTURE)

200 fleeces a day, removing each in as little time as 60 seconds, but a man must be an expert to keep this up. In 1957 an Australian champion sheared 327 sheep in a working day, but a New Zealander now holds the record, with 378.

It is difficult to cut the fleece cleanly from a wriggling sheep without nicking its skin. When the skin is nicked, a "tarboy" who stands waiting beside the shearing line is called. He paints the cut with tar or some other disinfectant so that it will heal quickly.

After the sheep are clipped they are herded into pens for counting and marking, and may be driven through a pool of medicated water in

Throwing the fleece to spread it out on the inspection table. (VICTORIAN DEPT. OF AGRICULTURE)

"Skirting" the fleece by trimming inferior wool from its edges. (VICTORIAN DEPT. OF AGRICULTURE)

order to kill any germs or insects that remain. Then they are sent out to pasture again, to start growing another crop of wool.

As soon as a fleece has been removed it is picked up by a helper, who throws it on a table so that it lies flat and right side up. It is inspected for cleanliness and quality, then tossed into a big bin containing similar fleeces.

When a bin is full, it is emptied into a giant press, which squeezes the wool into a bale inside a coarse wrapping. This bale, which usually weighs about 300 pounds, is then strapped. After it has been marked with the name of the woolgrower and with its destination it is ready to be shipped off to market.

Pressing the wool into a bale.
(AUSTRALIAN WOOL BUREAU)

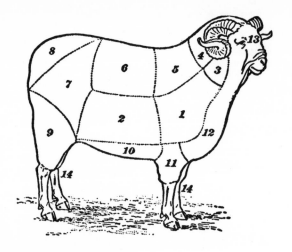

The numbers on the sheep show the order of preference for fibers — number 1, best; number 2, next best; and so on. (NATIONAL ASSOCIATION OF WOOL MANUFACTURERS)

VARIOUS KINDS OF WOOL

FIBERS OF WOOL vary greatly in length and in thickness, depending on the kind of sheep that produced them and on the part of the sheep's body on which they grew. Fibers from the sides and flanks are likely to be longer and coarser than those from the belly, which are usually soft and fine.

A fine fiber may be only an inch or two long and less than a thousandth of an inch thick. Coarser fibers may be three times as thick and from several inches to a foot or more long. The coarsest wool is used for weaving carpets and rugs, and comes mostly from sheep raised in the countries of western Asia.

Great Britain is famous for carpets, and much coarse, tough wool comes from the Scottish Blackface sheep, the most common wool variety in the British Isles. Blackface wool is sometimes mixed with finer fibers to make yarn for Scotch tweed, a rough, warm cloth that wears well and is excellent for making suits and coats.

26

Blackface sheep near Inverness, Scotland. (FARMER AND STOCKBREEDER)

An intermediate kind of wool which contains tough but finer fibers comes from sheep called crossbreeds. These are a cross between Merino sheep and coarse-wool English sheep, originally bred for mutton. New Zealand especially is known for its production of wool from crossbreeds.

The finest sheep wool, which makes the softest yarn, comes from the Merino. This yarn is especially good for making woolen underwear, in which no scratchy fibers can be used.

A typical Merino ram. (AUS-TRALIAN WOOL BUREAU)

Most sheep produce white wool, but there are breeds which grow wool that is gray, yellow, buff, brown, or black. Once in a while a family of white sheep has a black lamb. Remember the Mother Goose rhyme that begins, "Baa, baa, black sheep, have you any wool?" Over the years the words "black sheep" have come to have a different meaning, too. They refer to any person whose behavior is so unruly that he stands out from other members of his family just as a black sheep does in a flock of white animals.

The length of the fibers in a given fleece varies greatly. Before the wool is bought, it is necessary that an expert make a quick estimate of what proportion of the fibers will be more than four inches long, what part more than three inches, and so on. It is also important to estimate how much grease, salt, burrs, and dirt the fibers contain, in order to determine how many pounds of wool will remain after the fleece has been cleaned.

Wool being sorted into various types of fibers. (FELTERS' COMPANY)

PREPARING THE WOOL FOR SPINNING

WOOL AS IT COMES from the sheep's back is covered with a waxy grease that is made into lanolin, valuable for many purposes. Face creams are made from lanolin which has been washed from raw wool and purified. Lanolin is useful also in making lubricants, soaps, polishes, inks, and ointments. A pound of pure lanolin is often worth more than a pound of wool.

The process of washing greasy wool is called *scouring*. The raw wool is dumped into long vats filled with hot water that contains soap and other cleaning chemicals. Long metal forks are used to push the wool through several baths while the grease and dirt are gradually washed away. After this, the wool is sent through wringers and is finally carried on a moving belt through a long oven, at the far end of which it comes out dry and fluffy. Often, after it has been scoured, a fleece weighs less than half as much as it did originally. Each 100 pounds of dirty wool can be expected to give only from 30 to 80 pounds of clean wool.

If the yarn to be made from a batch of wool is to be changed in color, it must be dyed. When cloth of a single color is wanted, the dyeing can be left until after the fabric is woven, but when multicolored cloth in plaid, checked, or flowered patterns is wanted, the various yarns must be dyed either before or after spinning.

Wool can be colored readily by soaking it in hot water in which dye has been dissolved. To keep the color from fading after a while, the dye must be "fast," or permanent. The fastest colors are produced with dyes that penetrate the inner structure of the fiber material.

Coloring is now usually done by soaking the wool in large vats filled with hot solutions of dye. Great kettles with lids that can be clamped shut are used, so that steam pressure can be built up inside the kettle in order to force the dye deep into the wool fibers.

An old-fashioned spinning wheel. (MERRIMACK VALLEY TEXTILE MUSEUM)

SPINNING WOOL INTO YARN

THE OLD-FASHIONED method of spinning yarn on a hand-held spindle was very slow. It took weeks to make enough yarn for one coat or dress. Then, about five hundred years ago, the machine called a *spinning wheel* became common. It was made of wood and had a spindle which was turned rapidly by a string belt driven from a large wheel, rotated by hand or with a pedal. Loose strands of fiber ready to be spun were held on a forked stick called a *distaff*, and were fed onto the spindle by the spinner. The spindle both twisted the fibers into yarn and wound the yarn onto a spool, or *bobbin*.

A distaff for holding fibers while spinning. (GEORGE RUSSELL HARRISON)

The most difficult part of hand spinning is feeding the loose fibers to the spindle at a uniform rate so that the resulting yarn will be even in thickness and strength. These qualities can be controlled by varying the rate at which fibers are fed into the yarn and by the tightness with which the fibers are twisted together.

During the seventeenth, eighteenth, and nineteenth centuries, when England was the world's leading manufacturer of woolen cloth, many new machines were invented to speed up spinning and weaving. In most countries today these processes are done almost automatically by machines that operate at great speed. Millions of yards of yarn can be spun daily in a single mill, and as a result cloth and clothing have become much cheaper than they were in past times.

In large textile mills the wool is first blended, then sent through a *carding machine*, which combs all knotted fibers out of it. In carding, the blended wool is fed onto large rollers from whose surface thousands of tiny pins stick up. Smaller adjoining rollers with similar pins turn in the opposite direction, so each strand of wool is caught between oppositely

The tiny pins on the rollers of this carding machine disentangle the wool fibers. (U. S. DEPT. OF AGRICULTURE WOOL AND MOHAIR LABORATORY)

moving pins and is pulled straight. The wool comes out of the big rollers as a thin veil of fibers. A set of knives separates this veil into strips about one-half an inch wide. These strips are loosely twisted into soft, thin ropes called *rovings*, which are next wound onto large bobbins. A roving is so fragile that it will come apart if it is pulled hard.

Now the wool is sent through big spinning machines, each one carrying from fifty to one hundred spinning heads, all whirling rapidly. The machine unwinds the fiber bundles from their bobbins as it gives each

"French drawing" is the process that gives the wool a slight twist after it comes from the carding machine. Finished rovings are on the frame at the lower right. (EWING GALLOWAY)

Closeup of large spinning machines in action. (EWING GALLOWAY)

roving the extra twist it needs to turn it into a strong yarn. One operator can attend dozens of spinning heads at once, mending any yarn that breaks, and replacing bobbins as they are emptied or filled.

Many kinds of yarns are made, differing in diameter, twist, smoothness, color, and texture. Some yarns are spun to run lengthwise in a piece of cloth, while others are designed to make the cross-running yarns or to form patterns.

34

WEAVING AND FINISHING CLOTH

THE YARNS are woven into cloth on looms, some form of which is used by people of almost every country in the world. From the simple hand-loom of early times, on which only a short section of cloth could be woven by hand in a long day's work, large automatic machines have been developed on which cloth can be woven so fast that it grows several inches in length in a few minutes.

On a typical loom the long, parallel, lengthwise threads, called the *warp*, are stretched tightly side by side on a frame. A heavy wooden needle called the *shuttle* carries on a bobbin the crosswise yarn, called the *weft* or *woof*, which is to be interwoven with the warp threads.

To avoid the slow, old-fashioned method of interweaving the weft threads with the warp by passing the shuttle painstakingly over one warp yarn and under the next, a modern loom is arranged so that those warp

Warping worsted in a mill. In this process the wool is taken from the bobbins to form the warp, which is then wound around a cylinder called a warp beam.
(EWING GALLOWAY)

Automatic looms weaving a length of cloth. At the far right of the photograph the warp threads may be seen entering the loom. At the front of the same loom a piece of woven cloth can be seen, after the weft has been interwoven with the warp. (EWING GALLOWAY)

threads which the weft is to pass under can all be raised together by pulling a lever. At the same time, those warp threads which the weft is to pass over are left stretched underneath. The shuttle can then be thrown quickly between the two sets of warp threads, paying out its trailing yarn behind it. Then the second set of warp threads is raised while the first set is left below, and the shuttle is thrown between them in the reverse direction. So, simple weaving is done quickly and easily.

When various levers are pressed, different sets of warp threads can be lifted to let the shuttle fly under them at different times. In this way, patterns can be woven into the fabric, and cloth of different weaves can be made. If several shuttles are used, each filled with a yarn of a different color, and if first one set of warp threads is raised and then another, colored designs can be woven into cloth as it is being made.

36

Left: A drawing of one of the many weaving patterns, showing how the threads cross. (WOOL BUREAU) *Right: A loosely woven wool fabric.* (GEORGE RUSSELL HARRISON)

Many different kinds of weaves are used to make cloth for various purposes. In the simplest, called a plain weave, the weft threads go alternately over and under, then under and over, successive warp threads. Other weaves produce kinds of cloth which have such well-known names as twill, serge, flannel, tweed, and gabardine. There are many others, also.

Two types of cloth are woven from wool: woolens and worsteds. Worsteds, which have their name because they were first made in the seventeenth century in the English town of Worsted, differ from woolens in that they are more closely woven, from finer yarns, and have a smoother finish.

Other weaving patterns. (GEORGE RUSSELL HARRISON)

*Woven cloth on a loom,
a study in detail.*
(EWING GALLOWAY)

In yarn for woolens, many short fibers are allowed to stick out in every direction, resulting in the rough finish that makes fuzzy cloth so warm. Woolen blankets are sometimes made fuzzier by *teasing* the ends of some of the fibers out of the cloth with wire brushes, or with burrs from a kind of thistle called a teasel.

To make the harder yarn for worsteds, the short fibers, called *noils*, are separated from the carded wool by the process of *combing*. Noils are used in making woolens and felts. The long fibers remaining after combing are made into a *sliver*, or ribbon-like strand, known as *wool top*. In making worsted yarn the slivers are twisted more tightly than they would be for woolen yarn, so the resulting cloth has a smoother finish than that of a woolen, since all the fibers in it lie more parallel. Tweed and flannel are woolens, while serge and gabardine are worsteds.

38

Old engraving showing men cutting and fixing teasels to "raise" the nap on woolen cloth. (NEW YORK PUBLIC LIBRARY)

Old engraving showing workers "hand-raising" woolen cloth. (NEW YORK PUBLIC LIBRARY)

"Drawing" slivers of worsted. As they pass successively through rollers, each pair of which revolves slightly faster than its predecessor, the fibers are drawn lengthwise. (EWING GALLOWAY)

Woven cloth as it comes from the loom is rough like canvas, and may contain broken threads and knots. Workmen go over the cloth carefully, repairing weak places and replacing broken threads. Then the cloth is stretched so that its threads will lie flat and parallel — a process called *tentering* — and is cropped with high-speed rotating knives which trim off the fibers that stick out too far. Cheap cloth is sometimes *filled* with a powdery clay or a shellac, to make it denser and stiffer.

40

Tentering a piece of cloth so that it lies flat and is of uniform width. (FELTERS'
COMPANY)

Shearing the fuzz off the surface of a piece of cloth in a machine with rotating blades like those of a lawn mower. (FELTERS' COMPANY)

Articles of clothing that can be made to fit better if they are formed in one piece instead of being cut and sewn are often made by knitting. In this process a single yarn forms loops which are laced together lengthwise and sideways in chains to form a fabric. An area of knit cloth can be built up quickly by the use of big needles that handle the thread. The fabric can be made to take any desired shape by increasing or decreasing the number of loops in successive rows. Because they need to be smooth and stretchable, stockings and socks and sweaters are usually knit.

Machines knit garments much more rapidly than human hands can. Knit stockings were not invented until about the time of Queen Elizabeth I, in the sixteenth century. Before that, stockings were made from cloth, with sewn seams. They had no "give," and were very uncomfortable. Now, by using many needles, a modern knitting machine can make a stocking or sock in a minute or two. Each needle must go through seven motions to form the interlocking loops of yarn, but it does this faster than the eye can follow. A circular knitting machine can form a tube of yarn that has no seams.

It is fun to see dozens of knitting machines clacking together, each turning out sock after sock with scarcely a pause. When socks of only one size are being made, a whole bank of machines can keep on working hour after hour without adjustment.

WEAVING RUGS AND CARPETS

MOST OF THE RUGS and about half the carpets used today are made of wool. This is because wool fibers are tough and springy and hold color for a long time without fading.

Floor coverings that are to be walked on a great deal are different from ordinary cloth because they have threads running in three directions rather than in two. In addition to the warp and weft yarns that run parallel to the floor, a third set of yarns called the *pile* runs up and

A partially woven rug, showing the yarns of various colors and the sharpened wire needles over which the yarns are passed, leaving loops that are cut when the needles are withdrawn. (MERRIMACK VALLEY TEXTILE MUSEUM)

down. The pile makes a rug or carpet soft and thick and keeps it from wearing out for years, even though many people may walk on it.

The best carpets and rugs are made by first weaving a backing fabric of jute, cotton, linen, or some other yarn that is strong and not slippery on the floor, and then weaving into this the pile threads of wool, which carry the color and absorb the wear. In a very fine rug the pile may stick up an inch or more. So that it will not come loose, each pile thread is tied into the backing with a knot.

44

A closer view of the same rug, showing the pile and backing. (MERRIMACK VALLEY TEXTILE MUSEUM)

The pile is usually passed up through the backing and then down into it again, forming a loop. In some kinds of rugs this loop is left uncut, while in others it is cut so as to leave two pile threads side by side. In still others, after the rug is finished, the top of the pile is mowed smooth by a machine that operates like a lawn mower, with sharp rotating knives.

A rug differs from a carpet in that it is a piece of floor covering made in a definite size, and often has a complete design worked in colored yarns. A carpet is cut from a long roll of material or is made from a number of long, narrow pieces sewn together into the proper size and shape to cover a particular piece of floor. Carpets are usually tacked or cemented down, but rugs are movable.

45

Rugs came originally from the Middle East, where every Muslim has a prayer rug on which he kneels when he faces toward Mecca to pray. The desert Arabs of today spread rugs over the sand inside their tents. They roll up the rugs and carry them by camelback when the tribe moves. The Arabs' cushion covers, saddlebags, slippers, and wall hangings are all made of thick carpeting materials, usually of wool.

Most famous are the Oriental rugs which come from Iran (Persia), Turkey, the Armenian Soviet Republic, and China. Carpets and rugs are still being woven in these countries as they were ten centuries ago, on large and simple looms made of four poles onto which the warp threads are strung. After the backing has been woven, the pile threads are passed in and out through it and are tied by hand, leaving loops of uniform size. Putting in the pile is slow, hard work, for wherever a different color is needed in the pattern a new bobbin of wool must be used. Months of difficult labor often go into the weaving of one small rug.

Some rugs on display in museums were made as long ago as seven hundred years, although most of the best rugs are no more than four hundred years old. In former days, people were willing to spend years in making a single beautiful rug. One famous rug woven in 1540 and now in a London museum is said to have taken several weavers thirty years to make, for each square inch contains 380 knots tied by hand, and there are nearly 33 million knots in all.

Although the colors mellow with age, the designs in these old rugs remain bright and clear over the centuries because wool holds its dye well. During the Middle Ages many beautiful woolen pictures called tapestries were woven. These were made to hang on walls, to be admired rather than walked on.

Today most rugs and carpetings are woven on machines and are there-fore less costly. Two centuries ago a machine was invented in Brussels, Belgium, which looped an extra set of threads over a wire during weav-ing. When the wire was pulled out, a row of loops was left. When these

46

loops were cut, they left a soft, long-wearing pile. These Brussels carpets were sold all over the world.

Later a man named Joseph Marie Jacquard invented a way to make a loom weave intricate patterns automatically. He punched holes in cards in accordance with the pattern desired, and arranged these cards in his loom so that whenever a wire feeler struck a hole it would pass through and cause the loom to make a loop with a yarn of a given color. Separate wire feelers operated the bobbins which carried yarns of different colors. Although Jacquard's process was first developed for weaving silks, it was soon found useful for making carpets also. Because it was a much cheaper way of carpet manufacturing than others had been, many more people could now buy carpets. As a result, carpet manufacturing became a bigger business.

MAKING FELT

WHEN WOOL FIBERS are matted together, their scales become more and more entangled. This entanglement makes possible a process called *felting*. After the wool fibers have been softened by moisture, acids, and heat, they can be rubbed and pressed together to make felt cloth, a strong, smooth, bulky material that contains no spun and woven threads.

Felt cloth can be made in any thickness or size. Heavy felt is used to make thick pads for use under rugs and carpets and for cushioning machinery. Finer felt is used in making hats and as cloth for making skirts or jackets.

According to one story, felt was discovered accidentally by Arabs who stuffed wool under their horses' saddles when these rubbed sore places on the animals' bodies. Softened by hot and acid sweat, the wool gradually packed into lumpy sheets of felt. Another story says that felt was invented by a shepherd boy who stuffed wool into his shoes to protect his sore feet. Both stories may well be true.

Steaming felt to soften its fibers before it is sent through the felting machine, where the fibers are packed closer together by means of heat, moisture, pressure, and motion. (FELTERS' COMPANY)

Many large factories are devoted entirely to making felt from cut-up woolen rags and from noils, the shorter fibers combed from the wool that is made into worsteds. The finest noil fibers make the softest and best felt.

When a felt article that is not flat, such as a hat, is to be formed, a *batt* of wool much larger and thicker than the finished object is made. The material for one hat often starts out as a cone a foot and a half high and four feet around the base. This shape is built up by feeding successive webs of carefully prepared wool onto a rotating metal cone. One-half a

48

pound of fibers may be fed onto the form to make a cowboy's "ten-gallon hat" as a layer several inches thick is built up.

Then the wool is matted down by pressing and vibrating it in a closed box filled with steam. Large hammers may pound the felt to flatten and thin it while it is softened with acids. Shellac and other fillers may be mixed in to stiffen it. After some time this process produces a cone of thin felt densely matted together, which looks like a dunce's cap. This cone is pulled over a wooden block the shape and size of the finished hat and is then steamed by the felter as he stretches it in some places, compresses it in others, and works it gradually into its final form.

In finishing, the hat is rubbed with sandpaper to remove any fibers that stick out from its surface, its edge is trimmed to the desired shape, and sometimes decorations are sewn on. The felting process makes a hat that has no seams. Because the felt fibers can still be moved, the hat will gradually adjust itself to the shape of its wearer's head. When it gets dirty and out of shape the hat can be cleaned, then blocked by steaming and molding it on a suitable form.

Felt cloth made with dyed wool, coming out of the felting machine. (FELTERS' COMPANY)

WHAT WE LIKE ABOUT WOOL

THE NATURAL QUALITIES of wool fibers make for the soft fluffiness of woolen cloth, its toughness and resistance to tearing, and its ability to wear well and to hold dyed colors. The fineness and elasticity of the fibers, their natural curl and crinkle, and the scales they carry, all lend a share to these good qualities.

When moistened and heated, wool fibers become slightly plastic, so that they can be straightened or bent. Because of this characteristic a wool suit can be smoothed and brought back to its original shape when it is pressed with a hot steam iron. The fibers are softened by the heat and moisture and are moved into the desired position, where they harden as they cool.

All garments are likely to become wrinkled when they are tightly packed or actively worn. A "set" is put into the fibers wherever the cloth is sharply bent, especially when it is warm or moist. Such wrinkles can usually be removed from a woolen garment by leaving it overnight on a hanger in a warm, moist bathroom, where the wool fibers relax from the new sets they have taken and settle back to their former positions.

Another advantage of wool is that its fibers can stand high temperatures. Some textile fibers actually melt under the friction of the needle when cloth made from them is sewn rapidly, but wool does not do this. Neither does wool catch fire as readily as cotton or linen does. It tends to smolder slowly instead of bursting into flame.

Cloth made from wool does not unravel at its cut edges as readily as that made from other fibers, for the scales on the wool fibers hold them together. Again, woolen cloth stays cleaner than other kinds of cloth because the scaly fibers help keep dirt from passing into it.

Perhaps most important of all is the way woolen clothes keep their wearer dry. Drops of water are more likely to run off a woolen surface than to soak in as they do on the thirsty fibers of cotton. Even after the

50

An Arab in a black wool galabeah, *looking at the Great Pyramids of Egypt.*
(GEORGE RUSSELL HARRISON)

natural grease has been washed from wool fibers they have a waxy outer coating that keeps water from penetrating them readily. In addition, the inside of the fiber is made of a material that can soak up large amounts of water.

If a person's feet get wet when he is wearing heavy woolen socks, they

51

will stay fairly warm because wool can soak up quite a bit of moisture without becoming a good conductor of heat, and also because some heat is given out by the wool fiber itself when it accumulates water.

Although most summer clothing is made of cotton, linen, or synthetic fibers, strangely the same wool that keeps us warm is also good to keep us cool. When our bodies get hot we perspire — water comes out of the sweat glands in our skin and evaporates in the surrounding air. When this water is turned into vapor, the surface of the skin is cooled. Under a very hot sun, then, we need to wear clothes that will keep the sun's rays from shining directly on our skin and at the same time will not interfere with the evaporation of water from it. Woolen cloth not only has holes between its woven yarns, but between the fibers in the yarn and it absorbs much moisture. So woolens are increasingly being used for summer wear.

The Arabs and other peoples who live in the Sahara and Arabian deserts wear a garment called a *galabeah,* which keeps them cool in the daytime and warm at night. The *galabeah* is a loose gown often made of wool, which looks something like a long nightshirt and covers the wearer from his shoulders to his ankles. As the Arab walks, his gown swishes and pumps dry air up and down his legs. This air absorbs the perspiration evaporating from his body and carries the vapor away through the tiny holes in the woolen cloth.

WHAT WE DO NOT LIKE ABOUT WOOL

WOOLEN CLOTH has two serious drawbacks. It is likely to shrink whenever it is washed in hot water or with strong soap; and the grubs, or larvae, of several kinds of beetles and moths eat wool, especially if it is greasy or dirty.

Cotton shrinks only once, but wool keeps on shrinking every time the fibers get wet and are moved. A piece of woolen felt one hundred yards long has been shrunk to a length of only thirty yards. This difficulty

52

comes from one of the very features that makes wool so useful — the tiny scales on the fibers. Wherever two fibers with their scales pointing in opposite directions touch each other, the scales lock and, if the fibers swell and shrink, they move closer together. Scientists trying to find ways to keep wool from shrinking are experimenting with dipping the raw wool fibers in chemicals such as nylon, in order to give them a more slippery coating.

Today most woolen garments are dry-cleaned: dipped in chemicals such as purified kerosene, which contain no water and do not make wool fibers shrink. Sweaters are sometimes washed carefully with "cold-water soaps" so that the fibers will not soften and creep together. But we still need some inexpensive, easy way of washing grease and dirt from wool fibers without risking their shrinking.

Moths do not eat wool, but they lay their eggs in musty woolen garments hanging in dark closets. When the eggs hatch, the larvae eat all the keratin and grease they find around them — and at the same time eat the fibers containing the grease. So, moth holes often appear in woolen garments that have been stored. Moth preventives are useful only when they are put in among the clothes before the moths reach them, and when the storage space is quite confined. Even so, the moths and larvae, after many generations, are developing resistance to the odor of preventives.

Six kinds of moths and seven kinds of carpet beetles have larvae which eat about 100 million dollars' worth of woolen articles each year in the United States alone. If the larvae descended from a single female moth in a year all lived, they could eat 92 pounds of wool.

The best remedy is to mothproof woolen cloth when it is made. While the fibers are being dyed they can be soaked in chemicals which do not attract larvae and which will not be dissolved away when the cloth is washed or dry-cleaned. In this way, wool can be made even more useful to us all in our everyday lives.

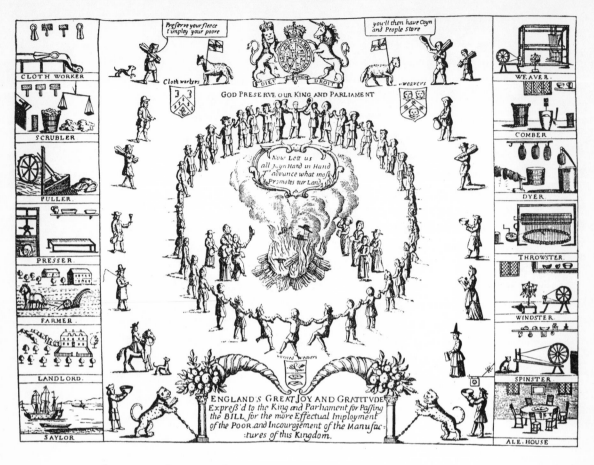

A seventeenth-century broadside praising the British wool industry and illustrating its processes. (NEW YORK PUBLIC LIBRARY)

THIS AND THAT ABOUT WOOL

UNTIL A FEW centuries ago wool was used in witchcraft, even in civilized countries. In parts of Scotland, bits of colored woolen thread were tied to cattle at Halloween to keep evil spirits from harming them.

In the Middle Ages it was thought that certain sicknesses could be cured by laying a piece of wool on the sick person's body, so driving the sickness into the wool, which was then burned. At late as 1600 a doctor in Scotland prescribed black wool and salt as a remedy for any disease.

As recently as 1825 it was an offense punishable by death to take sheep out of England to be sold. At that time the sheep and wool industry was the basis of England's wealth.

To help sell more English wool, one king ruled in the sixteenth century that everyone more than seven years old must wear a cap made of wool whenever he went out of doors, or pay a fine of about 80 cents for each offense.

Since the sixteenth century the Lord Chancellor of England, the country's highest judge, has sat on a woolsack, or pillow stuffed with wool, whenever he was carrying out the business of the court. Formerly, all persons who swore loyalty to the king were required to kneel on a woolen cushion while doing so, to remind them of wool's importance to the kingdom.

Some terms commonly used in everyday speech come from the wool-growing industry. "Woolgathering" is a word that comes from the practice of gathering stray tufts of wool that have been caught on thorns and bushes in the pasture. Now it means idle, purposeless thinking or inattentive daydreaming. "Woolly-minded" means vague and fuzzy in thought. "Hard to tell the sheep from the goats" is a phrase that indicates the difficulty of separating valuable things from those not so valuable.

55

WORDS USED IN THE WOOL TRADE

ALPACA — A soft cloth made from the wool of the alpaca, a small relative of the camel that lives in South America.

BATT — A mass of wool ready to be shaped into a felt hat or other article of felt.

BLENDING — Mixing together fibers of various types to obtain wool suitable for some special purpose.

BOBBIN — A container for wound yarn.

CARDING — A process by which wool fibers are disentangled after they are cleaned.

COMBING — A process for separating the shorter fibers from the longer ones which are to be made into worsted yarn.

CRIMP — A fiber's natural curves, which make a resilient yarn.

DISTAFF — A stick on which a mass of fibers is held to be spun.

EWE — A female sheep.

FELT — A kind of cloth made without weaving, by matting hot, moistened fibers of wool until they cling together closely.

FILLING — Adding powdered clay, shellac, or other materials to raw cloth to increase its body, stiffness, or density.

FLEECE — The pelt of wool fibers growing on a sheep, or sheared from a sheep.

HAND — The way a piece of cloth feels when it is handled. This depends on its fluffiness, body, and texture.

KERATIN — A chemical substance produced in the bodies of many animals, of which their hair, hooves, horns, or nails are made.

KNITTING — A process of forming cloth from one or more yarns by interlacing loops with knitting needles.

LAMB — A young sheep.

LANOLIN — A substance refined from the waxy grease that covers the surface of each wool fiber as it grows on the sheep, and used in making cosmetics, lubricants, and ointments.

Llama — A relative of the camel that lives in South America and gives coarse wool that is made into cloth.

Loft — That quality of wool which measures its ability to make soft, thick, and warm cloth.

Loom — A device for weaving cloth, on which the warp threads are stretched lengthwise so that the weft threads can be interlaced at right angles to them.

Merino — A breed of sheep widely raised in Australia and elsewhere, which produces a heavy yield of wool of high quality.

Noils — The shorter fibers combed from wool preparatory to making worsted yarn. They are used in making woolen yarn and felt.

Pile — The fibers that stick up from the surface of a rug or carpet to make it soft, resilient, and long-wearing.

Processing — Processing begins after the wool has been sheared from the sheep's back, and includes scouring, drying, carding, combing, spinning, and dyeing.

Ram — A male sheep.

Roving — A bundle of parallel fibers slightly twisted to hold them together before spinning.

Scouring — Washing wool to cleanse it of grease and dirt.

Shearer — A man who shears the wool from sheep, usually with power-driven clippers.

Shuttle — A device that moves back and forth across the cloth as it is being woven on the loom and pays out the weft thread behind it.

Sliver — One of the narrow ribbons into which the thin layer of wool is sliced as it comes off the carding or combing machine.

Spindle — A device for twisting wool into yarn.

Spinning — The process of twisting a bundle of fibers to form a yarn or thread.

Staple — A measure of the length of the fibers of wool.

Teasing — Pulling out loose ends of fibers so that some will extend from a woolen yarn to make it fuzzy.

Warp — The threads that run lengthwise in a piece of cloth.

Weft, or Woof — The threads that run crosswise in a piece of cloth.

INDEX

DATE DUE

FORM 393 SCHOOL SPECIALTY SUPPLY, SALINA, KANSAS

2/11/70			
2/18/70			
3/58/70			
45 - 4 -72			
5-13-85			